Primix Publishing
485c US Highway 1 South
Suite 100
Iselin, NJ 08830
www.primixpublishing.com
Phone: 1-800-538-5788

Published by Primix Publishing: 08/19/2024

ISBN: 979-8-89194-243-1(sc)
ISBN: 979-8-89194-244-8(e)

Library of Congress Control Number: 2024913591

Wealth

101

Impacting

2 Generations

PRIMIX
PUBLISHING
THE WRITE CHOICE

Acknowledgements

Paul (passed) and Ros my parents much love, thanks for making me the man I am today.

To my lovely wife, I will always love you Nicole. January 24, 2024 was the start of our separate assignment, you are forever in my heart and mind.

Brenda Blake "Lady B" you did a great job raising this wonderful and beautiful woman of God.

Nick, continue to be the man God called you to be.

Kingston, I can't wait for you to become a "King".

My siblings, Rosa Brown, Tyrone VanDyke, Paulette VanDyke and Rodney VanDyke thanks for the love and support. Martin Williams, my mother beyond blood, much love.

New Community Church, much love, the best is yet to come.

My teacher and coaches at Smithfield High School, Chowan University, Liberty University thanks for the push, I will never stop learning.

To all my teachers, mentors and instructors, family and friends, thanks for your patience, I want to make you proud. Each day I will strive to become a better version of myself. Each day, I want to strive to reach the unreachable and discover things that we never thought about.
Life, you are teaching me new things each day. I will never take you for granted.

Thanks to Anya and Anna Williams for your creative direction and design for the book cover, your brought to life my intentions for this project.

Sign

Amp.

Contents

2 Generations

Proverbs 13:22
"A good man leaves an inheritance to
his children's children, but the sinner's
wealth is laid up for the righteous."

While writing this manuscript, the light went on for me. According to Proverbs 13, we are to leave wealth for 2 generations. Wow! What a different perspective on money and how we are to become good stewards and leave the world a better place than we entered.

I challenge you today to start living beyond yourself and setting up the next 2 generations. For many people, this is a stretch. Life is difficult trying to maintain what you have and staying above water is hard enough. You can do it, you

and his son Solomon. King Solomon inherited his father's throne and his relationship with God. Notice I said, King Solomon knew God because his biological father had a relationship with God. Parents, we must make sure our children understand the power of God and give them the opportunity to have a working relationship with God.

Money is great, but passing on a deep spiritual relationship with God can produce dividends beyond our understanding. We must understand it is God that gives us power to get wealth. All it takes is one revelation, one idea, one sign from God and your life will never be the same.

Scripture is saturated with instances where God takes one act of obedience and changes the lives of many forever. Having a 2 generation mindset is about following the plan and path of God. He will direct you and give you clarity on how to move forward. Once I adopted this saying, my financial disposition changed for the better. Repeat the statement below and adopt it as your own. "Money

 is Easy, Obedience is the Challenge." The scripture that makes this saying a reality is Matthew 6:33 "But seek first his kingdom and his righteousness, and all these things will be given to you as well." Seeing is believing. Let's start this chapter with honesty and humility about our financial competence. It doesn't matter how you learned about finances, you saw it and it stuck.

"You saw, therefore you believed, that it was either your financial road map for success or your financial pitfall." With nearly three decades in the financial industry, I have witnessed numerous people raised with a poverty mindset.

 What I mean by poverty mindset, is people that are bad financial stewards repeat what was taught to them and what they see. It may seem strange but seeing is believing. People repeat what they see, children duplicate what they see in adults. It's hard to erase what you see on a daily basis. Bad stewardship can be passed from generation to generation, just like a last name.

I remember getting that first allowance and running to the local candy lady, who sold snacks real cheap. It is absolutely amazing what you could purchase with .25 now that doesn't cover the taxes. I'm sorry food is my weakness, I don't want to bring you into my world, I am a recovering food addict. LOL Unfortunately, if the parents had bad credit and no savings, the children will follow that same pattern. There are exceptions, but for the most part they repeat what they saw and experienced from their parents.

Today, we break that generational curse and create new expectations and understanding about money and wealth. I am a witness that the cycle can be broken. My father was a hard working man that provided for his family. I can clearly hear my father say, "I want you to be better than me." Paul VanDyke, had a third grade education, but the most intelligent person I have ever met. He never made excuses, he taught his children the importance of hard work. My mother Rosa knew how to stretch a dollar to make sure we were good. We didn't have a lot of money but it never felt like we were poor. All our needs were met, we had enough. There is something to be said about having enough and simply being ok with that. While the previous statement might seem contradictory to creating wealth, as I have matured in life, my driving force for wanting to become wealthy is to make the world a better place.

I'm sorry I keep drifting off the subject, back to what we see is believing. We adopted that philosophy and made the best with each opportunity given to us. In addition to working hard, I grasped the reality that wealth is possible. Just believing that wealth is possible is half the battle. Being trapped in a poverty mindset will keep you captive and under performing your entire life, if you allow it. Take a deeper look around you, there are people doing big things in your present circle. For example, the first wealthy person I saw and experienced was the local ice cream man. Mr. Dave owned the ice cream truck, local baseball team, local nursing home, local small convenience store, lots of real estate and countless other businesses. Many of my friends called Mr. Dave a hustler, he had his hand in many things and he was a blessing to our community.

I came to realize is Mr. Dave saw an opportunity in our community and he provided services at a fair price. This was major, I soon came to realize more is possible if you are willing to step outside the box. Mr. Dave thought outside the box, when he saw an opportunity, he dived in.

Opportunities are all around us, many have not trained and are noy prepared to see them. What do I mean, they are all around us? We see that we prepared to see. When you live in life in expectation you find yourself discovering what you believe is possible.

Same goes those who believe nothing good ever

happens to them. It's amazing they get what they subconsciously believe they should have in life. Ok let me address the elephant in the room. Yes you may not have people in your life that believe more is possible. You don't have an excuse, we live in a world where information is available 24/7. The power of AI has changed the way we get and gather information. You can change right now!!!! the internet is full of people that have big visions. Stop spending all your time watching unproductive TikTok and find people who are living your dream. When you find people that are living the life you desire, you should make that your priority. Investigate who made it and begin to follow that recipe for success. Now that we know that seeing is believing, let's get ready to start from ground zero. I named the next chapter ground zero, because I believe that wealth is available to all people. Some may have to work harder than others, but it is possible. Let's go to the next chapter ground zero.

Ground Zero

A 2 Generations mentality is not beyond reality if you see ground zero as your training ground. You don't have to start with a silver spoon in your mouth. Wealth is available to all, some just have a harder journey than others. My father Paul VanDyke, Jr. and my mother Rosa weren't highly educated people, but they taught us the importance of working hard.

America is the greatest country in the world. People are risking their lives trying to cross the border to get an opportunity to be successful. The American dream still exists for those who believe it is possible.

Not everyone will be rich, but we can be better. The purpose of this book is to put a fire under all those that want more from life. This book will give you simple tips and advice on how to maximize your current financial condition and become monetarily savvy so that you may find your wealthy place in life.

When I say wealth, I am not just talking about money. I have been in the presence of many that had money but were poor. Are you ready to start your wealth journey? If so, I need you to be open minded and teachable for the next few hours of your life.

In the next chapter, we will start with the money IQ. Please answer those questions with honesty and sincerity. It will help you understand your current position on money. If you are going to be a 2nd generation person, it's time to test your money IQ and if you fail, there is time to get the needed information to prosper and make a difference in the lives of those you love the most.

Let's Go!!!

Money IQ

1. Who taught you about money?

2. Who taught you how to spend money?

3. Who taught you how to save?

4. Who taught you how to invest money?

5. Who taught you how to earn money?

6. Who taught you how to bless people with money?

One of the items below is considered an asset and the other a liability.Butter or Gold? What is the difference?

Butter- sneakers, cars, designer clothes etc. Gold-Stocks, savings, 401k, real estate Yes, you should reward yourself, but not to the point where you do not have any savings.

Lower middle class to poor people own more butter than gold. We break the vicious cycle today. Who cares how much Louis Vuitton you have? A Roth IRA is much sexier than those red bottoms that will depreciate the minute you walk on them. No matter where you are in life you can start the journey to accumulating wealth. You must be willing to divorce yourself from all the wrong things you know about money. Unless you came from high financial status, understanding the principles of wealth is a foreign language.

Wealth is not a conversation most people that look like me talk about. Today we will start that conversation. When eating Sunday dinner at Big Momma's house we are NOT talking about wealth, retirement, entrepreneurship, building a legacy and creating financial freedoms for generations.

The Mind and Money

Most people do not need more money, they need to transform how they think about money. Once the mind is transformed, your bank account is affected immediately.

Question:

If you made $100k and spend $98k, you net $2k.

If you make $30k and spend $25k, you net $5k.

Who has more money?_____

Power to Get Wealth

Deuteronomy 8:18

But you are to remember the LORD your God, for it is He who is giving you power to make wealth, in order to confirm His covenant which He swore to your fathers, as it is this day.

God gives you the power to obtain wealth.

God gives you the power to obtain wealth.

    a. Knowledge

    b. Know how

    c. Information on how to obtain money.

    d. Information on how to maintain money.

    e. Having the expectation that more is available.

Wasted Money

When you waste money, you are canceling the future of 2 generations. It is not about you; it is about those we leave behind. Ok. We talked about 2 generations. Here is what I have noticed about those that are sincere about leaving generational wealth, all their needs are met. You cannot leave generational wealth and be personally broke. "Money given to undisciplined people is wasted"

According to the National Endowment for Financial Education, 70% of lottery winners go bankrupt within a few years. Obtaining more money often leads to careless spending and the desire to get more money.

How much do you need to be comfortable?

If money were no issue, what would you be doing? Wealth defined? An abundance of valuable material possessions or resources.

Wealth provides freedom and flexibility in life.

The Big Misconception

Time=Money?

They are both valuable, but time has the greater value. Money can be produced and reproduced, but "time" once it has gone it cannot be replicated.

"Poor people trade time for money"
"Wealthy people produce money to have quality time."

Example
I stopped cutting my grass. Initially I felt bad, until I realized I hated cutting grass. I now use that time to do other things that can produce revenue. One of my business partners often say, "what is the highest and best usage of your time." Once I came to that realization, life changed for me.

The Value of a Minute

When people ask if I have a few minutes the answer is really know, since I know the value of a minute, let us do that math.

$100,000 annual salary

$1923=per week

$48=per hour wage

$.80=per minute

Wasting 20 minutes a day x 5-day work week x 52 weeks a year=$4166 per year wasted.

- The above calculations are based on a 40-hour work week.

Types of Income that accumulate wealth.

2 Generational wealth is about generating income that puts you in position to leave an inheritance. You should have streams of income. Never get comfortable with what you have always strived for more. Here is a scripture that supports sources of income. In the Garden of Eden one river became four sources that flowed. Genesis 2:10 And a river went out of Eden to water the garden; and from there it separated and became the source of four rivers.

No One is Exempt from the Wealth Journey no matter your income. Grow from where you start. This chapter is for those who did not grow up with a silver spoon in their mouth. Wealth 101 is about understanding where you are, then maneuvering to improve your financial condition. When your money starts working for you, wealth accumulation begins to take place. I want to start with the most basic income to the more complex one. Surveying adults from all levels of society, ignorance about money, finances and wealth is common among most people, no matter how much money they make. Most people without hesitation say they need help. Here is a list of the most

basic income to the more complex income streams. I am not sure where you are, but wanted to include all occupations and all kinds of financial situations. The truth is that you can grow from any place you are right now. This is not the time to be embarrassed. Let us learn something, here is a list of incomes:

- Welfare
- Social Security
- Disability
- Hourly
- Salary
- Pension
- Workers Compensation
- Buy and Sale on Internet
- Commission Sales
- Business Owners

- Day Traders
- Investing in Crypto Currency
- Dividends from Investments
- Buying and Flipping Houses
- Residual Income from Real Estate

The greatest income not mentioned is information. Going forward, you should treat information as currency. When you get information, and you respect it, change is around the corner.

After I reached my late forties, I began to extract information from successful people that understood finances. A common thread among wealthy people is their yearning for information. Wealthy people often surround themselves with smart, articulate, and competent people.

What is the importance of those characteristics?

a. Smart People realize they need to change. They realize money is a tool, not a pillow. A tool is used to build, construct, and make the world a better place. Money used properly will change your life and impact generations beyond our lives. A pillow mindset causes you to trust your money and it gives you false security that you "made" it. Pillow mentality will cause you to be stingy. Stingy people do not live in faith nor overflow, take notice.

b. Articulate People, they can express what they want. Change only happens when you know what you want. Knowing what you want allows you to eliminate what does not correspond with your vision and goals in life.

c. Competent People, I love these people, they execute the game plan. Competent people do not make excuses, they find a way to increase income and live a better life. Competent people refuse to be the victim. Wealth is about moving beyond your financial condition and taking the responsibility to be financially fit.

Paycheck to Paycheck

Understanding how to save money from each paycheck will change your finances immediately. Once I captured the understanding of not spending everything, it changed my life.

Stop: Before you say if you made more money, you would have more money. Not true. In my business, there are clients that make north of $250,000 and they have less than $20k in savings. On the other hand, I have clients that make $50k annually and they have 15k in savings and checking.

Is the problem money or discipline? It is a discipline problem. Follow me, let's answer some questions.

Are you living paycheck to paycheck?

_____

How much money do you have now?

_____

How much money do you waste?

_____

Do you realize most people that are good financial stewards have excellent credit, is this a coincidence? Why?

_____

Do you have Margin?

What is Financial Margin? Having a healthy financial cushion allows you the freedom and flexibility to be live a comfortable life without the stressing about how to make ends meet.

Do you often feel like you deserve something because you work hard?

Do you have margin in your life?   _____

                                                    _____

Do you normally have margin in your
finances?   _____

                                                    _____

_____

Did your parents have margin?   _____

_____

Do your friends have margin?   _____

How much are you willing to save the next time you are paid to increase your margin.

Simple Tips to Create Margin

2 Generational wealth is about creating margin. When you create margin, it allows you to save for the next generation. Margin is not about surviving but thriving. People that have margin in their lives have at least five of these vehicles that create margin, notice you have enough to start today.

Plastic Milk Carton

Rolls of Coins

Piggy Bank

Safe for cash at home

Checkings Account

Savings Account

Emergency fund

Christmas fund

Vacation fund!

401k

Stocks

Crypto Currency

Mutual Funds

Primary Residence

Second Home

Investment Property

Your Work and job or Career

Is having a job bad?

No.

As long as:

A. It creates enough income to meet your needs and provides a savings for the future.

B. It is your passion, and you would almost do it for free.

C. If it is your passion, create a business and duplicate what you enjoy.

D. Are you making a difference in the universe? When you have influence, a legacy is created, therefore future generations will benefit. Wealth goes beyond money; it is providing a level of financial security that allows those you love the most to live a maximized life.

Your best investment is in yourself.

Why should others care more about you than you?

What books are you reading?

Who is doing what you desire to do?

Who is mentoring you?

Are you strong enough to accept them being honest with you?

When you invest in yourself it produces:

A. A life that allows creativity to flow.
B. A life that is lived without limits.
C. A life that is lived without financial restraints.

Wealthy people solve problems.

Wealth is created from those who solve problems. Solving problems is bigger than disgruntled people. The marketplace is full of problems, waiting for the next "Joe" to do something about it. Here are a few problem solvers.

1. Steve Jobs   -Apple
2. Bill Gates   -Microsoft
3. Jeff Bezos   -Amazon
4. Mark   -Meta (formerly
   Zuckerberg   Facebook) (FB.)

5. Eric Thomas   -On demand
                        Motivation

Once you find the gap, you create a wealth stream. The problem with most people is that they have been trained in a poverty mindset. The poverty mindset keeps you stuck in that dead end job, wishing and hoping that things get better.

Now for some, people their 9 to 5 provide an

exceptionally good income. They can save, pay bills, and live a good life. I am not talking about that person. I am talking about the person who complains about not having money and doing nothing about it.

The bigger the problem the more you can demand. Problem solvers aren't special, they just don't settle.

Not all businesses are wealth makers. Take the time to find a need and address how to solve it.

Wealthy people create jobs

Please understand you can do a business while
Please understand you can do a business while
require lots of capital, to find and solve a
problem, your capital investment may become
minimal.

For example,

Realtor/ Broker
Mortgage lender/Broker.
Compensation for higher production model,
opposite of hourly or salaried positions.
General Contractor
Real Estate Investment, Primary Residence
to investment every two years or Fix and Flip.

Owning a daycare, being different, providing private tutoring, etc.

Athletic training facility connected to a school system, specializing in strength and conditioning.

Owning a franchise or creating your own brand to franchise.

Trucking Business

Sharpening your skills, getting the highest paying job in your field. They will pay you more. Lawn Care-lucrative, specializing in seasonal plants, lighting for all seasons, there are no luxury lawn people in this region.

RideShare seniors, medical transport, quality vehicles and dependable employees you will service out among the competition. Tax services and accountants, seasonal but highly profitable.

Lucrative Government contracts or government employees retire and get another pension.

Use over time as a savings account.

401k is free money.

Stop lending money, get a financial advisor, and start saving today. No matter how broke you are

now, you can save something. The problem is you lack discipline and you have accepted not having money is part of who you are and what you do. Become a bargain person, you do not pay full price for anything. It is the two fish and five loaves
concept.

Succession Planning

As we conclude this instructional manual, this last chapter is extremely important. There must be a succession plan in place. Wealth left to an undisciplined financial mind will be squandered within a generation. Without a succession plan, all the sacrifice and financial accumulation is for nothing. I remember working at a car dealership and watching several people spend their entire inheritance on new Dodge Chargers. That was insane as I think about it now.

As a 55-year-old father and grandfather, my heart is torn as I think about what the deceased sacrificed to leave an inheritance. We must work equally hard in planning our successor. When I think about a succession plan several families come to mind, the Walton family (Walmart), the

Vanderbilt family, the Rockefeller family, The Kennedy family and the Ford family, just to name a few.

The common denominator is there was a person waiting to assume the family business and keep financial momentum going. The good thing about momentum is you add energy to what is already in place and moving.

Those that carry off the succession plan, don't feel a sense of entitlement, they feel a sense of responsibility to continue what was started. I am not an expert on succession planning, just want to inform you of its importance.

In conclusion, without going too deep, we know who will keep this moving and who will destroy what has been established. Trust your heart, it will guide you into all truth as you appoint your successor.

Finally, have fun as you begin to create wealth that will impact 2 generations. You owe it to those that follow, let's leave the world a better place. Remember it is God that gives us the ability to get wealth. Ask, Seek and Find, is your next step to creating wealth that will impact 2 generations.

Financial Glossary

Wealth 101 provides the basic concept of money and develops your mind to operate at a higher level of financial competence. There are terms you need to understand.

Assets-a useful or valuable thing, person, or quality:

Budget-is a spending plan-based n income and expenses. In other words, it is an estimate of how much money you will make and spend over a certain period, such as a month or year.

Credit-the ability of a customer to obtain goods or services before payment, based on the trust that payment will be made in the future: ("The Basics of Credit")

Debt- a state of being under obligation to pay or repay someone or something in return for something received: a state of owing.

Financial Margin-is having extra after you pay your debts. Margin provides a financial buffer in the event of an emergency. It takes discipline to maintain a stable margin.

Income- Money you receive from doing work or financial gains you receive from investing.

Generational wealth is assets that are passed down from one generation to the next, such as money, property, or a family business.

Money-is any item or medium of exchange that symbolizes perceived value.

Wealth-abundance of valuable material possessions or resources